Reflections:

Daily Stories of Inspiration, Motivation, Encouragement, and Planning

Warren I. Jaycox

Published by White Cottage Publishing Company
Website: http://whitecottagepublishing.com

Interior and Cover Design: Tom Mack, MBA
White Cottage Publishing Company

Cover Photo by
Warren Jaycox and Tom Mack
Photo of Author on Back Cover Courtesy of
Rick Ouellette Photography
http://www.rickophoto.net/
Rohnert Park, California USA

To contact the author or to order additional copies of this book:
Online: E-mail: warren.jaycox@whitecottagepublishing.com

Printed in the United States of America for Worldwide Distribution
ISBN: 9798563913233

DEDICATION

This Book Dedicated to:
Jeanette Marie (nee Woods) Jaycox
May 12, 1937 to November 9, 2020
63 years of encouragement and love.

Acknowledgments

I am indebted to so many people who not only inspired me but encouraged, assisted, advised, and sometimes cautioned me as I put fingers to the computer keys. I wish to recognize them and thank them, not blame them for the final result.

I want to thank Dr. Paul Muresan, who got me directed into serving God in so many ways. I thank Dr. Eugen Jugaru for his support and encouragement of establishing Vacation Bible Schools (VBS) in several Pentecostal Churches in Romania. He and his wife Dana and children Thea, Laura, and Cristian welcomed me into their family during my visits to Codlea, Romania; occasionally three and sometimes four times a year. Although I had received the usual Methodist baptism back in 1932, Pastor Jugaru baptized me by immersion in a ceremony at his church a few years ago. It was an indescribable spiritual experience.

I learned a lot about writing from classes taught by Deb Carlen. I hope she is pleased with the final result of her so often errant pupil. I am indebted to the late Jo Reeves (may she rest in peace) and Tom Mack, who edited my first two books and nurtured them through publication. Again, Tom has kept me focused on completing this project. His suggestions, his ideas, and his contributions made this book considerably better. I am forever thankful.

Sonoma VBS Team members Claire and Bob Jones, Kymry Borkenhagen, Megan Hall, Nancy Ouellette, and Ardath MacDonald have always been encouraging to me and dedicated to the VBS program.

Many others supported my efforts by proofing, commenting, and providing ideas for additions, modifications, and deletions. I am listing them as I can recall, not in any particular order. Sylvia Lofftus, Paula Lofftus, Flo Beth White, Ardath MacDonald, Dr. Ryan Rindels, Lisa Cole, Diane and Henry Mayo, Sharon Richards, Diana Sirois, Russell Jaycox, Bradley Jaycox, Jeanette Jaycox, Lorena Moldovan, Theodora Lupien, Ica Jugaru, Nick, Petru, and Dany Gligore, Narcis Murza, Debora Murza, Cristina Necoliu, Perrin Heaverin, Jessica and Doug Schiller, Amanda Stanbro...

Inevitably, I have omitted a dedicated person(s) that should be recognized. I humbly request their forgiveness and understanding. My elevator doesn't go all the way to the top anymore.

Warren I. Jaycox
Sonoma, California
November 12, 2020

PREFACE

Some books just seem to happen. I didn't intend to write this book, but like life, things happen.

It all started back in 2004 when I had my first experience as a volunteer on a Vacation Bible School (VBS) team heading to Romania. The leader, Paul Muresan, and his assistant Diane Johansen had a dynamic program that resonated with the children and inspired me to continue working as a VBS team member.

In 2012, I wrote a book, *Organizing and Operating a Vacation Bible School Overseas* and the follow-up publication *Have You Started Yet?* All of this experience led me to start a blog that I published weekly for 18 months. As I reviewed these blogs with an editor, Deb Carlen, she exclaimed that I had the makings of an inspirational book.

Thus started a four-year process, on-again, mostly off again, of putting this book together. I utilized some of the blogs as-is and others with appropriate rewriting. I've included many personal experiences of myself and other members of my team. I like to think they are God-inspired. Then, some vignettes ask you to assess where you are in your Christian life and perhaps challenge you to seek a closer relationship with God.

One day in Fagaras, Romania, a local team member confided in me that I was an inspiration to him. I cherish that comment more than many other honors bestowed upon me. I pray that my messages herein will to inspire you as well.

To help my readers, I have left many blank pages in this book so they can make their own notes, ask questions, or just doodle.

Other Books by Dr. Warren Jaycox

*Organizing and Conducting
a Vacation Bible School Overseas* (2012)

Have You Started Yet? (2014)

Coming Soon:

The Adventures of Sebastian, the Cat.
An audio-book for children.

Vacation Bible School (VBS) Made Simple
An updated revision of previous VBS books.

TABLE OF CONTENTS

Day 1:

How Do We Know When We Arrive?

Our usual practice following the traditional Sunday dinner was to take a ride in the family car. So I said, "Let's go." Amid squeals of joy, everyone hopped up and headed for the car.

Everyone, that is, except my son, Russ. He looked at me inquiringly.

"Where are we going?"

I have to admit, I had a secret destination in mind, but I said,

"We're just going to drive around."

Then came his zinger,

"But how will we know when we get there? If we only drive around with no destination, aren't we just spinning our wheels? If we don't know where we are going, how will we know when we arrive?"

This is not an uncommon question. A group of people, family, work, church team, for example, can get excited and anxious, ready to go, with no clear understanding of the destination. Worse yet, each person can have his/her concept of the ultimate destination or goal.

To get focused, you need a plan. God didn't just say, begin, and everything fell into place like pieces in a jigsaw puzzle. God created everything in an orderly, planned fashion, one day at a time for six days.

"Wait," you say. "He took seven days."

"OK, but He didn't create on the seventh day, He rested."

If planning was necessary to God, perhaps we should learn from His example.

Here are some planning steps that parents and leaders of small or large groups of people can use to keep them charged up, full of enthusiasm, ready to go, and headed for the car?

- Involve the family/group/team in the goal-setting so they will see the benefits of reaching the goal.

- Define each step toward the goal in simple, easily understood terms

- Make progress measurable and observable.

- Establish a timeline showing do-by dates for each step. You not only need to know where you are going, the route to get there, but when you'll arrive.

I know that sounds like I'm complicating things. On the contrary, the more you can define your way, the easier the trip.

You may find large rocks in your path that cause you to stumble. Look at them as ways to test your determination. Life's like that sometimes.

There is a time when family members may want to "drive around." That is family bonding time. Spending relaxed moments with the family is as vital as an intense group effort on a project. Build bonding time into your plan.

My secret destination?

The favorite family ice cream parlor. Yummm.

I will instruct you (says the Lord) and guide you along the best pathway for your life; I will advise you and watch your progress.

—Psalms 32: 8 NIV

The more you can define your way, the easier the trip!

Day 2:

When Things Go Wrong

Murphy's Law says that if anything can go wrong, it will... There are just days when it seems that nothing goes right!

My first clue was the aerosol can of shaving cream didn't shut off when I lifted my finger off the spray button. Shaving cream shot forth everywhere. It was a new can. There was shaving cream on the mirror, all over my face and hands and the floor. In desperation, I put the relentless spewing can into the shower, closed the shower door, and cleaned up the mess.

Fortunately, I always allowed extra time in my morning routine for unexpected occurrences so I wouldn't be late for work.

In my hurry to get dressed, I inadvertently put both feet into the same trouser leg, lost my balance and fell, bruising my hip and twisting my knee, so it was painful to walk.

I tried to keep a positive thought. Even though my day started off wrong, I would cheer up. After all, it could be worse.

Sure enough, it got worse.

During breakfast, I didn't notice the cat had up-chucked on the floor by the coffeemaker. I stepped in the slippery mess and tumbled once more, spilling coffee on my shirt, tie, and the wall behind the now coffee-stained breakfast table. In the process, I bruised my other hip and severely strained my right wrist so I couldn't write.

I had only been up for an hour.

I don't have days like that often, but those days do happen.

If you ever have days like this, stop for a few moments, take three deep breaths, and remember:

> *Trust in the Lord with all your heart and*
> *lean not on your own understanding; in*
> *all your ways submit to him, and he will*
> *make your paths straight.*
> *—Proverbs 3:5-6 NIV*

Unexpected and hindering events may continue to plague you during the day. Do not lose heart. Don't feel you are in a helpless state. This is my command – be strong and courageous! Do not be afraid or discouraged.

> *Have I not commanded you? Be strong*
> *and courageous. Do not be afraid; do not*
> *be discouraged, for the LORD your God*
> *will be with you wherever you go."*
> *—Joshua 1:9 NIV*

Together, you and God, Make it a good day!

Do not be afraid; do not be discouraged, for the LORD your God will be with you wherever you go. (Joshua 1:9b NIV)

Day 3:

Your Church –Temple or Tomb?

Everything dies sooner or later. People die, businesses die, plants die, pets die, organizations die, even churches can die.

Why do churches decline in membership and eventually die or join with another barely surviving church in a desperate hope to stay alive? The obvious evidence of this is that new members are not replacing members who:

- become infirm, unable to attend, or die,

- must leave because of a job change relocation

- have a family relocation,

- feel the focus of the church on God has changed.

- feel the church leadership is weak and aimless

- dislike friction between member factions of the church

- have other personal priorities

If you have ever left a church, you probably have a reason that you could add to the list.

To more fully understand what happens to a dwindling church, ask this question: Why do people go to church anyway?

A thorough answer to that question still plagues many a pastor and church leadership. Here are some, but most certainly not all, of the reasons a person may attend church:

- ✦ They want to have fellowship with God.

- ✦ Going to church is something Christians do on Sunday.

- ✦ They want to be seen doing Christian things, want to have a Christian persona.

- ✦ They like the social atmosphere and have many friends there.

- ✦ They enjoy serving God by being in the choir, teaching Sunday School,

- ✦ They have a leadership role as deacon, elder, governing board, and so forth.

- ✦ They feel they get status in the community by being a church member/attendee.

You may be associated with a church in its infancy, with maybe ten members, a small church, say average attendance of 35, or with a large church with membership in the hundreds. I have even attended a megachurch of thousands of members, with immense TV screens to enable the multitudes to see the pastor clearly.

Does size mean you get closer to God as a congregation increases? There may be added attractions such as a choir or band, Sunday school for all ages, personal opportunities for missions both local and out of the area, even overseas. If a person desired to be a participating, involved member, there is something for everyone. Do these trappings, despite their value, become an end in themselves. Where does Christ fit in?

Is the mission of your church, regardless of size, great or small, Christ-centered? If it is, you are in a temple. If not, it will become a tomb.

Christ says, in Matthew 18:20 (NIV),

> *For where two or three gather together*
> *because they are mine, I will be right*
> *there among them.*

Did you feel that way the last time you worship in your church?

In other words, a church is a collection of people with Christ-centered lives serving God. As such, the church should be full of love and welcoming people.

What are you doing to help your church be that kind of church, one that will never die but will continually prosper for the Lord?

Can you do more?

God loves us the way we are, but too much to leave us that way.

Day 4:

I Hate It! I Won't Do It! No Way!

I hate this job! I hate it! I hate it! I Hate cleaning out storage areas. And I bet you do too. Last week, I was cleaning out a storage area, one of the things I had been saying I was going to do, but always finding excuses to delay. I had to be in the right frame of mind to make countless decisions.

- ✦ What do I want to do with this?
- ✦ Is this in the category of keep?
- ✦ Do I put it in the **can't decide** pile?
- ✦ Where's the trash can pile?
- ✦ Decisions. Decisions. Decisions.

While I dislike sorting through mostly **Junk**, there are parts I enjoy. For example, I just uncovered the **treasure** box. I call it that because it is equivalent to a special artifact that archeologists hope to find: an artifact from which they can determine how the person lived, what he/she ate, maybe even how the person died.

I picked up a miniature plastic piano I could hold in the palm of my hand. Memories flooded back to when Mrs. Moore, my fifth-grade teacher (and also a music teacher) awarded me that prize for being the best in the class at finding smaller words in the longer word she wrote on the blackboard every morning.

That was the first thing this troublemaker ever received for excelling at some acceptable behavior. It felt good. And as I held this little award in my hand, those same feelings came back. Toss this out? No way!

Sorting through old treasures is hard, very hard. These are not practical items that allow me to say, *If I didn't use it in the last six months and don't think I'll use it in the next six months, then it out it goes.* But the items in the treasure box are different. **It is hard to toss out an item that has good memories attached.** You know what I am talking about, don't you?

The next item I touched as a note I got from my boss at my first job. It was a brief handwritten note thanking me for my help on a particular task. He didn't have to do that, but it meant a lot to me. All those past events came cascading back as I sat in a dreamlike trance, just me and my memories.

I smiled, a big broad smile from ear to ear as I recalled all the thoughtful people who have been part of my life.

Then I searched my mind for thoughtful actions I have taken for the people around me in my life. Oh! How negligent and insensitive I have been! Am I alone in vowing to correct these failings?

What have you been doing that will put a piece of you in someone's treasure box?

Who knows what items from you are going to bring happy thoughts and a big smile to someone's face?

It is hard to toss out something that has good memories attached to it.

Day 5:

They Said, "Don't Do It!"

It seemed as if everyone was advising us not to do it. We received phone calls and visits from relatives urging, no, pleading with us not to go. Now, looking back many years later to 1957, the idea was foolhardy at best; this desire of headstrong young newly-weds, to fly across the country from El Monte, California to a small town of Marshfield, Massachusetts.

I had just earned my private pilot license and had only 48 hours total time, only eight hours past the minimum. I was young full of confidence that I could achieve anything.

Members of the flying club I had joined while I learned to fly, had only these words of advice:

+ Don't fly in bad weather!

+ Don't fly at night!

Good advice for a brand new, over-confident pilot...

The adventuresome duo (my wife and I) held hands, said a brief prayer for a safe trip, and took off heading for the first stop in Phoenix, Arizona. As we made a farewell sweep above the airport, we were astonished by what we saw.

My Wife and I Embarking on Our First Trip Across the USA.

Sitting brazenly at our airplane parking spot was our car, doors wide open. Was this a bad omen of things to come? We safely landed, parked the car, and made another attempt to start our trip.

After an hour, we noticed clouds were beginning to accumulate as we flew over the Colorado River. As we continued across Arizona and New Mexico, the clouds got more ominous and very dark.

The sun was setting. It began to rain. So much for following advice!

In the direction of our destination, the sky was almost black. Foreboding and scary only begins to describe it. Flashes of lightning danced around the sky over El Paso, our destination for the day.

I radioed the airfield requesting weather conditions at the field. I was still 30 minutes away. The tower operator suggested an alternative airport at Deming, New Mexico.

I quickly searched my sectionals (air maps). My lack of experience was beginning to show. I had neglected to bring adjacent sectional (map) showing Deming, New Mexico, so I radioed for verbal directions. The tower operator gave me a heading to fly from where I thought I was.

The radio reception was abysmal. The last words I could understand were,

"Caution the mountains on your right."

Then nothing but static amplified by an occasional flash of lightning.

Below us was a rocky desert of undulating hills. I could barely make out a dirt road beneath us.

We had been on this course for over fifteen minutes. Darkness was closing in and the rainfall was more intense. It was decision time. I had three choices:

1. Continue to fly and hope to find the airport.

2. Land, and weather out the night and the storm.

3. Fly into the mountains.

It was starting to rain harder. I made a decision,

"Say a prayer, Jeanette, I'm going to try to land on the road."

Just as I pulled the throttle to descend, Jeanette exclaimed with excitement,

"Look, over there! "

Way off in the stormy, dim distance, I could see the rotating beacon of the airport.

God was showing me the way out of danger. God's beacon was our salvation.

Now, as I recall this incident, I think of the troubled lives many people must have. I think about how lucky I am to be able to show them the beacon of Jesus Christ. I can tell them that despite the darkness, how stormy their lives may be, Jesus is the way!

One of the joys is that we can serve as a beacon for Christ. We can shine our light on a way through the troubles of life by accepting Christ as our Savior.

As we model our life on Christ's example, we become beacons for others.

Let It Shine! Let It Shine! Let It Shine!
Who is the beacon in your life?

Day 6:

Plan for Success

"The vast population of this earth, and
indeed nations themselves, may readily
be divided into three groups. There are
the few who make things happen, the
many more who watch things happen,
and the overwhelming majority who
have no notion of what happens."

Dr. Nicholas Butler, 12th President of
Columbia University, March 1931, Charter
Day Speech at the University of California

Sally was a young, happy, loving wife and mother
of two delightful children. She was comfortable
with her duties as the family homemaker. That all
changed when she agreed to chair the Holiday Fair at her
children's school.

Sally had always been a **Watcher**; now, she must be
a **Maker**! This was a new role for Sally. But Sally was a
mature lady and didn't try to **tough it out**. She recognized
she needed help, so she sought out the president of the
Parent's Club for some guidance. Sally thankfully received
these helpful comments and suggestions.

"He who fails to plan is planning to fail."

Winston Churchill

Develop a plan using these techniques:

1. Contact people who have had the experience before and get their suggestions. Learn from them, both the good and bad thing that happens.

2. Go to bookstores and Internet sites such as Amazon to see what materials and books you feel may be helpful.

3. Do Internet searches using Bing, Google, Yahoo, and other search engines. They can provide leads to information that may give you some guidance in your project.

There should be an item four. Pray for God's guidance and support. The plan you develop will be for material guidance. You should ask for spiritual guidance as well.

You see that his faith and his actions were working together, and his faith was made complete by what he did.

–James 2:22 NIV

Using your research, make a chart using four columns. Column One is Task to be done. Column Two is how many people involved. Column Three is what materials and supplies will be needed, and column Four is labeled space required. I say to make a chart because an essential step of any plan is putting your thoughts in writing.

Task	People Required	Materials/ Supplies	Space Required

This chart will show you the people necessary to operate the Fair, the materials you will need, the supplies you will need, space you will need. From this information, you can extrapolate the funding you need. Yes, this becomes very detailed, very specific. But it is crucial.

Putting everything on paper removed the struggle of trying to keep all the balls bouncing around your mind. You will feel more relaxed and in control of your situation.

> *Never be lacking in zeal, but keep your*
> *spiritual fervor, serving the Lord.*
> *–Romans 12:11 NIV*

You have a detailed plan that gives you all the requirements, down to the needed tables, chairs, paper clips, masking tape, staples printers, and so forth.

Remember the five "Ps:"

Proper planning promotes praise-worthy performance.

Day 7:

If He Asks for One Mile, Give Him Two

My wife and I decided to take our dream cruise along the coast of Mexico. Cruises are nice. You pay the fare and put your money away. Eat as much as you want, when you want and where you want because there are places to eat almost everywhere on the ship. Relax in the sun, enjoy the caressing ocean breeze and watch the world go by...

There are drawbacks, however. Not many, but one soon learns to adjust. Consider communications, for example. To send an email, it is necessary to connect to wi-fi someplace. You guessed it. Someplace is the ship. The ship will sell you Wi-Fi time so you can communicate by phone or email like a busy corporate magnate. But it is expensive.

Time flies when you are having fun, and it zooms when you are using email. One week, I sent three emails, and got a bill for over $40. A fellow passenger told me he waits until the ship gets to port. When he goes ashore, he finds a bar, coffee shop, or maybe an Internet Café. Some charge a minimal fee; others have no charge but expect you to buy something like a cup of coffee, a soft drink, or even an alcoholic beverage.

The next time the ship docked: I scurried down the gangway to the dock, along the lengthy pier, to the money-hungry port facilities and businesses. Needless to say... I was anxious to begin my search mission for a Wi-Fi location.

Luckily, I readily found a bar/coffee shop/restaurant offering free Wi-Fi! I ordered a Coke and went to work, sending out e-mails and sipping my Coke. Life should be so good.

Then it happened!

When the waitress brought my bill, I reached for my wallet. It wasn't there. I had no money. Most cruise ships have a small safe in each cabin for personal valuables like passports, jewelry, and money. In my desire to start sending messages to those at home, I had, unfortunately, neglected to grab some money.

Various scenarios went through my mind:

+ Walk back to the ship and get some money. No, because I would still leave without paying.

+ Offer to leave my cell phone as security, then go and get my wallet. Good idea except the ship was due to sail before I could get back.

+ Admit my stupidity and convince the cashier I was weird by offering to send the two dollars by Western Union as soon as I got home in a week.

+ Swallow my pride and ask some other customer to lend me the money to pay my bill.

Many patrons sat enjoying their refreshments who looked like they could be shipmates, but I didn't recognize anyone.

Sheepishly, I approached a nearby table. Hesitant to interrupt the conversation, I just stood there. Finally, I spoke to a lady with a kindly face and explained my predicament. She looked at me and said something I couldn't understand. I thought of a famous line from an old W. C. Fields movie,

"Go away, kid, you bother me."

22

Sensing my embarrassment, another person at the table motioned me over and asked me, in a friendly tone, what I wanted. Once he understood my plight, he reached for his wallet and handed me 50 pesos, more than enough to pay the bill. I introduced myself. His name was Roger. I attempted to get his ship cabin number so I could repay him, but he waved me off and wished me a safe and happy journey.

> *Whoever is kind to the poor lends to the LORD, and he will reward them for what they have done.*
> *–(Proverbs 19:17 NIV)*

Afterward, walking thankfully back to the ship, I thought about how much the local community and church volunteers were like Roger. They see a need and act without hesitation. They give willingly in abundance. They do all this without expectation of reward. It is the right thing to do. Roger gave from his wallet; the volunteers give from the heart.

You're right. Roger gave from the heart too.

To overcome anything,
one must start –
and proceed,
one step at a time!

Day 8:

Odessa

Odessa was an active member of the church I attended, always involved in overseeing or sometimes even leading a church project. I recall that for several years she was the enthusiastic person spearheading the drive for Christmas Shoeboxes. They were just that, shoeboxes, but filled with items that were appropriate for boys and girls in some overseas country who needed a gift at Yule time. One year, under her charismatic urging, the congregation donated over 500 shoeboxes, way beyond anyone's expectations.

That was Odessa. She always had a smile and a warm embrace for everyone. She was a grandmotherly type of person. One could rightly say that she was a bustling bundle of love.

> *For if the readiness is there, it is*
> *acceptable according to what a person*
> *has, not according to what he does not*
> *have.*
> —*2 Corinthians 8:12 ESV*

For over a quarter-century, I have received traditional size greeting cards from Odessa, a lady I hardly knew. These cards were unusual, to say the least. Each one was handmade, personalized with an appropriate message. Be it Thanksgiving, Christmas, Father's Day, birthday, or just any day; the mail might include a special message from Odessa.

A widow, she had problems of her own. She didn't talk about it, yet we all knew she had a mother in Oregon in poor health and other family members that she would travel to visit frequently. In recent years she quit commuting to Oregon and moved there. But that didn't stop the greetings from Odessa.

Still, the envelopes come with her words of love and encouragement. When my wife's health declined to the point that she needed total care, I placed her in a senior care home. Odessa's expressions of Christ's love followed her there, a time of joy for my wife when the cards arrived.

Odessa had a constant saying that was an essential part of the handwriting on every personalized card: **Remember that He cares!**

Somehow Odessa divined when it was time to send me one of her unique, personalized cards, like the occasion when I was having a devastating case of *poor me*, and her card changed my attitude 180 degrees.

I've never discussed this with Odessa, perhaps I should. Obviously, this is her personal ministry for Christ, one that has helped hundreds of people over the years. I considered trying to do that too. But I guess my calling is to serve the

Lord in other ways. Odessa has her calling. I have mine. What is yours?

> *Blessed be the God and Father of our Lord Jesus Christ, the Father of mercies and God of all comfort, who comforts us in all our affliction, so that we may be able to comfort those who are in any affliction, with the comfort with which we ourselves are comforted by God.*
> *— 2 Corinthians 1:3-4 ESV*

What can you do to help someone else feel brighter, feel loved, feel that He cares?

Acts of Kindness are contagious. Help Kindness to develop into a pandemic!

Day 9:

Bible Frustration

Sometimes I get unbearably frustrated, like having an itch that won't stop when I scratch. What causes such unceasing frustration? The car refuses to start... No. The toothbrush battery dies before I finish brushing... No. My wife won't admit I'm right... Not this time.

My frustration was with the Bible!

It is not fair to place the blame on the Bible because it is entirely my fault. Let me explain.

My daily routine starts with reading a minimum of five chapters of a book in my Bible. After I brew my tea and settle on the couch, I begin reading from where I left off the day before. Today I read in Romans 7:15, 19 (NIV):

> *I do not understand what I do. For what I want to do, I do not do, but what I hate I do... For I do not do the good I want to do, but the evil I do not want to do—this I keep on doing.*

I find this passage, as I do many others, difficult to understand, so I have to read it several times to get the meaning. But it is not the word order or the context that bothers me. It is what happens to me when I read a word or phrase that brings to mind some weakness I have. Unconsciously, I stop reading, recall situations, and daydream. Perhaps it is my sinful nature, my past catching up to me. It impacts me because I feel the Bible is talking directly to me.

> *The unfolding of your words gives light;*
> *it gives understanding to the simple.*
> *—Psalm 119:130 (NIV)*

I don't think I am alone in this frustration. Haven't you ever had a time in your Bible reading when you paused, unconsciously, thinking of the opportunities you could have grasped and didn't; or were faced with temptations to overcome and did or didn't succumb.

Does it bother you to read a passage that brings back memories of Christian failings? It does to me, more often than I would like. But those times are becoming less and less bothersome as I have grown older and try harder to practice my faith. I can recall more times now that I kicked Satan's butt than I could as a young man. I have had Christian successes too.

Over the years, I have read the Bible many times, and each time I have fewer shameful thoughts and abundant good thoughts. God's message is becoming evident to me.

> *To God belong wisdom and power;*
> *counsel and understanding are His.*
> *—Job 12:13 (NIV)*

God was showing me that all my mental diversions were His way of helping me understand His teachings. I understand and accept the wisdom of His subtle guidance.

Now I can see the folly of following my own way, not His, and the unfortunate results.

As you read your Bible, and I hope you do, take your time, enjoy the diversions, seek to understand the message, and savor a closer relationship to Christ.

Don't let frustration be an obstacle to progress and understanding.

Day 10:

Be a Short-Term Missionary

"Think of all the starving children in China!"

That was my mother's mantra when I left any part of her scrumptious meal in front of me. I pictured distributing my uneaten food to some emaciated, deprived children in China as my mission contribution. Yes, I thought of them, and they could have it, all of it!

Missionary life was portrayed as a lifelong endeavor when I was a youth. In recent years, different kinds of mission experiences are possible. Now, people can be missionaries for varying periods, sometimes as short as a week, although two-three weeks is more common. Also, there are different types of mission needs in locations all over the world.

Just imagine a small team of two to three individuals or couples from your church going to a country overseas to help with evangelism projects like a vacation Bible School, a small construction project, or other humanitarian activity. An Internet search of *short-term missions* will display the possibilities. A slowly  emerging trend is for a church to conduct its own short term overseas mission.

Go therefore and make disciples of all the nations, baptizing them in the name of the Father and of the Son and of the Holy Spirit.

-Matthew 28:19

What attracts a person to the adventure of a short-term mission?

+ They become focused on missions, not just any **mission**, their mission.

+ **Mission** emphasizes the evangelical nature of being a Christian. Members can exercise their faith and get to circumstances where they literally **live** their faith.

+ They get a chance to interact with people of other cultures. In some cases, it may be possible to live and eat with them.

+ They can show their love of Christ through their interaction with the children and volunteers with whom they work. For example, a Vacation Bible School (VBS) team.

+ They get an opportunity to form a closer bond with other members of their mission team.

+ They have the opportunity to use vacation time for a Christian purpose, not just personal enrichment and enjoyment.

+ They open themselves up to a life-changing experience.

+ They want to do something that can make a lasting difference in other people's lives.

What can be a better motive than that?

If you have ever been on a mission, you know the positive effect it had on your life and how you now feel as an enriched Christian. If no one in your church has proposed involvement in a short-term mission, that's because no one has stepped forward and asked for God's help and proposed the idea. Why not you? Somebody must do it. Why can't you be that somebody?

Think about it. Talk about it. **Pray** about it.

Make it happen!

Be for somebody what you want somebody to be for you, Awaken Your Destiny!

Narcis Joel Murza

Day 11:

Attention by Intention

Where does Christ fit into your daily routine? Perhaps I should have asked IF Christ fits into your daily routine.

Maybe a better question would be, "Where does Christ fit into your life?" Or does Christ fit into your life? Most people who claim to be Christians say He is part of their daily life. If that's the case for you, does it show? Does your speech and routine interactions with others reflect your Christian life, your Christian manner?

How often do you think about doing something for someone else, a relative, friend, or acquaintance? It also could be for some unknown individual whom you contact just because they are a part of some group you support, such as the Red Cross or the Salvation Army?

I thought of a former neighbor the other day. I miss him a lot; we were always swapping stories, tools, often helping each other with a project. I should drop him a line, I thought, but then didn't do it. Have you ever had similar thoughts, to let someone know you care? Maybe I'll write to him this afternoon. Yeah, sure.

In some cases, when we get around to it, they are gone, never knowing how meaningful their life and friendship were to us. **A personal note now is much more treasured than a flower on the coffin.**

I readily confess that I am far from perfect. I often refer to myself as a recovering sinner. More often than not, I can be considered a bad example. For instance, I have an uncle-in-law named Henry. He is 92 years old, a widower, and can, fortunately, still live alone. Imagine, if you can, his lonely existence. I think of him often, but what good does that do him? I should contact him and reminisce about the fun times we shared, like the day on San Pedro Island beach when he attempted to …well, you get the idea.

Like many people, I have a lot of good intentions. In my case, before I can call, write, email, or visit Uncle Henry, an unanticipated force requires my immediate action. Suddenly, my needy relative is way down on my priority list, maybe even forgotten for a while.

When is the last time you thought of where the people in need are on your hierarchy of priorities? Who is your equivalent of Uncle Henry? A former classmate? A parent, grandparent, or intimate friend?

Tomorrow, after your daily Bible reading, give your **Uncle Henry** your *attention by intention!* Intend to put that personal contact first. No excuses. *Just do it!*

Download your worries; get online with God.

Day 12:

Greetings

Ienjoy sailing on cruise ships. I don't care what ports they visit; it's the lifestyle I relish. There's just a lot that I like about cruising. I love having someone make my bed, clean my room and bathroom. If I am hungry, a wide variety of appetizing food is available. If I want to exercise, a walking or jogging course and a place filled with unique exercise equipment beckon me.

Other attractions are the library with fiction and topical non-fiction books, varied enticing activities during the day, theater entertainment in the evening, a pool, hot tub, water slides, climbing walls, and numerous music venues, just to name a few.

There is, however, another reason most cruises are irresistible to me. It is not some physical attraction or shipboard activity. The priceless benefit is a happy, cheerful, positive atmosphere.

Interestingly, the cruise line doesn't seem to make a difference.; when I leave my cabin and meet anyone of the crew, regardless of their job or status, I receive a cheerful greeting. As I walk along the corridor, everyone, irrespective of how busy they are, greet me appropriately. Wherever I go, crew members will always say something pleasant to me, be it on deck, in the elevator, in the dining room, virtually anywhere we meet.

The ship staff wants me to enjoy my life aboard their ship, starting with a warm smile and a heartfelt greeting. I'm not sure that they genuinely feel that way. Perhaps they had a bad night, had a fight with a good friend, or don't feel right, but they put on a smile and say something that makes me want to smile and respond in kind.

For example, yesterday, as I was walking outside on one of the upper decks to bask in the sunshine, I came upon a member of the crew who was busy painting. The painter didn't ignore me as I walked by. He said, " Good afternoon. Isn't it a nice day."

In conversations I have had with ship personnel, I have never heard a complaint. Oh, I'm sure they have complaints, everyone does, but they also know I don't need any additions to my burden bag.

Do you have something positive or cheerful to say to everyone you meet? Do you smile even when you're hurting inside? Are you ever too busy to give a smile, a wave, a "hello" to someone? Larry, my neighbor, is never too occupied. This morning he was on the far side of his driveway, involved with some car repair. Larry could easily ignore me without offending me, but, like always, he said, "Hi, Warren, How's it going? Larry brightens my day!

How many days do you brighten for people? Why not make it a habit for yourself always to have a good thing to say to everyone you meet. Be a beacon of good cheer. And know this, when you give encouragement, show love, or concern, you are helping them, and like a lively ball, good cheer will bounce right back to you.

> *And the King will say, "I tell you the*
> *truth, when you did it to one of the least*
> *of these my brothers and sisters, you were*
> *doing it to me!"*
> *—Matthew 25:40 NLT*

Smiles beget greetings; greetings beget friendships, friendships beget love; let love beget a peaceful world.

Day 13:

Attacking Tasks

The alarm rattled to life at the ungodly hour (for me anyway) of six o'clock in the morning. That's 0600 for those of you who prefer military time or the 24-hour timepiece.

I tried to erase my sleep thoughts or dreams from my mind and concentrate on all the things I needed to do today. As was my habit, I had made a written "to do" list before my prayers last night. I reread the numerous items, mainly a series of daunting tasks. Every day I woke up to things I didn't want to do. One day, I simply said the heck with it and went back to bed.

But avoidance is not a wise solution.

It would be a rare person who could claim that they never experienced such feelings.  Many would say that this was the miserable way they started their day. Can you relate to this experience? Consider how Moses must have felt when he had to back up Mt. Sinai to tell God that he had broken the tablets of the Ten Commandments... Intentionally. He was furious at the people and lost his cool.

Perhaps you can recall the story in Exodus 32:19 (AMP):

> *And as soon as he came near to the*
> *camp he saw the calf and the dancing.*
> *And Moses' anger blazed hot and he*
> *cast the tables out of his hands and*
> *broke them at the foot of the mountain.*

Don't you think that Moses dreaded going back up Mount Sinai?

The natural tendency is to put off the task you dread, the one you would put off until tomorrow if you could. Guess which task headed Moses's list?

> *I feared the anger and wrath of the*
> *LORD, for he was angry enough with*
> *you to destroy you.*
> *—Deuteronomy 9:19 NIV*

Moses didn't put it off. God instructed Moses to prepare two more tablets and come back up the mountain. (Exodus 34:1) It turned out that God wasn't mad at Moses; God was mad at the people. Scratch #1 off Moses to-do list.

Make your list in order of difficulty. Put the one you want to avoid at the very top of your list.

Put the next least desirable task next, then the next undesirable one, and so forth. Don't place what you consider the easy one first. It will get done in good time

By tackling the perceived worst problem first, you are more alert. You are more energetic and clear thinking. More often than not, the matter will not be as bad as you anticipated. You were geared up mentally for the big game and ended up with a scrimmage. Don't fear the first item. Do it, then move on to number two. You should feel refreshed because to have made it through the biggest problem of your day. Think about how Moses must have felt.

Armed with confidence, number two isn't as bad as you anticipated, either. It could have been worse, but you were ready for it. Having overcome problem two, move on to number three, then four, and by the time you reach the bottom of the list, you will be surprised how much time you have left.

Be strong and courageous. Do not be afraid or terrified because of them (tasks) for the LORD your God goes with you; he will never leave you nor forsake you.

—Deuteronomy 31:6 NIV

Don't let fear rob you of the outcomes you desire. Walk with God toward the light at the end of your tunnel of despair.

Let your faith be bigger than your fear!

Day 14:

Milestones of Life

In 2006, I experienced a milestone event in my life. At least I see it that way. Milestones are those events in one's life that signify a steppingstone on the journey across our stream of being. They are events in our life that represent a time when our life took a turn, where our life made a shift in direction, intensity, and pace.

Well, you say, isn't everything that happens to us a milestone?

That depends... If those events don't have a significant effect on your life, they are just pebbles in the stream. Most people would list birth, starting school, change in family status, graduation, marriage, the death of a close one, getting a job, or losing a job. You could fill up pages writing the milestones of your life.

Like most people, I have had many landmark situations. Some I would like to forget but cannot; others I cherish more and more as time rolls by.

One of my most precious memories occurred when I decided to join a Vacation Bible School (VBS) team going to Romania, a new experience for me.

It happened when I was attending a worship session in an auditorium in Calan, Romania. Over 600 VBS children were praising the Lord. Gradually, I noticed a little girl about seven years old, and from appearance, was a *roma* (gypsy). As such, she was culturally rejected by the general population.

She had climbed into the seat next to me and was fascinated by the hair on my arm. She began to stroke my arm. As I gave her a welcoming smile, she leaned against my side. I gently took her hand. Despite all the noise and activity around us, she fell asleep.

She didn't know me, I didn't know her... yet at that moment, there was a Christian bond between us. She was quite thin. Did she have a family? What was her home situation? I didn't know. But I did recognize that she was feeling acceptance, security, and the love of Jesus Christ flowing from me as she slept on my arm.

That was a milestone moment for me. When I felt a warm glow of happiness surge through me, my decision was made. It has been a good one; to continue to work actively with and for VBS programs.

In a town I had never heard of, that little *roma* girl, turned the focus of my life. Hundreds of children and countless volunteers have come to know the Lord because of that little gypsy girl and the ever-lasting effect she had on me.

Some people never experience a religious milestone. I will hazard a guess that one good reason is that the person avoids the steppingstones across God's stream. Or maybe they take a step on the first stone, then maybe the next and the next but then stop. Could it be they are over halfway across and don't want to go further because that might mean commitment?

They may go to church and participate in the worship service, but that is all. Honestly, they are a bench warmer. They want to feel part of the team but don't relish getting in the game. Perhaps they tithe or at least donate in the offering plate or bag. Could that be a ransom for inactivity?

Do you risk situations where you might be asked to do more, to do something to help the church or others, wherever they may be?

I believe that we all have some little gypsy girl who needs love and attention. But you have to be where she can find you. Remember, I didn't find her; she found me. When you feel touched, you will know it.

By being touched, I mean experiencing a special feeling, so different than ever experienced before. A feeling so good that you want to experience it again. And again. I get that feeling when I kiss my wife, even after 63 years.

I felt the touch when I began singing in the choir as a young man.

When I was called to present the morning devotional to the VBS team, it was only ten minutes, but when members of the team told me later, they had been inspired, I was touched.

I realized that happiness is best experienced when my life activities, events, conditions, and circumstance are not centered around me but are focused on others. I hope that is true for you too.

Listen to what God is trying to say to you. And don't just Listen but **Hear** and **Heed** His calling.

Happiness is felt best when it is centered around others rather than yourself.

Day 15:

Should and Did

It is difficult to understand the Book of Numbers in the Bible. Please take a minute to think about what the book is telling us. I know this is hard because Numbers can be a very dull book because of its insistence upon reciting statistics that may not mean much to us now. Despite that, the Bible, so far, has tried to tell the people with Moses what they **should do**. In Numbers, we read what they **did do**!

For example, when Moses and the people got to Canaan, the land the Lord had promisesd them, the Lord told Moses to send twelve men, one from each tribe to explore the land. After 40 days, they reported back.

> *They gave Moses this account: "We went into the land to which you sent us, and it does flow with milk and honey! Here is its fruit. But the people who live there are powerful, and the cities are fortified and very large. We even saw descendants of Anak (the giants) there...*
>
> *And they spread among the Israelites a bad report about the land they had explored. They said, "The land we explored devours those living in it. All the people we saw there are of great size. We saw the Nephilim (the giants) there (the descendants of Anak come from the Nephilim). We seemed like grasshoppers in our own eyes, and we looked the same to them."*
>
> *—Numbers 13:27-28, 32-33 NIV*

Joshua and Caleb, on the other hand, returned with a different, but "Minority Report,"

> "The land we passed through and explored is exceedingly good. If the LORD is pleased with us, he will lead us into that land, a land flowing with milk and honey, and will give it to us. Only do not rebel against the LORD. And do not be afraid of the people of the land, because we will devour them. Their protection is gone, but the LORD is with us. Do not be afraid of them."
> —Numbers 14:7-9 NIV

As revealed in the Bible, God tells us what is right, and thus, we know the opposite, what is wrong. In the over 2,000 years since Moses, it seems we haven't learned much. We continuously struggle between right and wrong. In practice, that is, through life, we get to know what is right and develop lifestyle, cultural mores, and thinking so that we do the right thing naturally. Well, most of the time.

But not always.

Apostle Paul expressed it well in Galatians 5:16:

> For the flesh desires what is contrary to the Spirit, and the Spirit what is contrary to the flesh. They are in conflict with each other so that you are not to do whatever you want.

Do you ever feel this way? Such feelings can lead to despair, frustration, and even depression. You don't want to be there.

Paul realizes he has a sinful side that is in constant turmoil with his desire to do good. Paul is no different from all of us.

So how can one avoid such disastrous effects? Christ offers us redemption from the cross. Paul also said:

> *Those who are dominated by the sinful nature think about sinful things, but those who are controlled by the Holy Spirit think about things that please the Spirit. So letting your sinful nature control your mind leads to death. But letting the Spirit control your mind leads to life and peace.*
>
> *—Romans 8: 5-6*

An alcoholic can learn to control the urge to drink, and you can learn to control the urge to sin. Ask God for help and set your mind to curb your urge to sin, one day at a time, for the rest of your life.

You can do it. Will you?

If you answered, "I'll try," that's a cop-out response. I recall a scene in the famous move: *Star Wars: The Empire Strikes Back* when Yoda told Luke Skywalker to do something. Luke answered that he would try. Yoda emphatically said,

"There is no try! Do!"

During World War II, the Navy construction battalions (Seabees) had a hard-earned and well-deserved motto: CAN DO!

Members of the armed forces today will tell you, The difficult we do immediately, the impossible may take a little longer.

You see, try infers you accept that failure is possible. You have an excuse that you tried; that allows you to give up too soon. Don't do that. Have the mental focus that you can; then do.

Once again. With God's help, will you set your mind to curb your urge to sin, one day at a time?

God, help me be the person you know I can be!

Day 16:

The Recovering Sinner

If there are key elements in Christianity, they are Christ's death on the cross, forgiveness of sins, and His resurrection. Apostle Paul says in Colossians 2: 13-14:

> *You were dead because of your sins and because your sinful nature was not yet cut away. Then God made you alive with Christ, for he forgave all our sins.*

When Christ died for our sins on the cross, He gave us the opportunity to have our sins forgiven if we just come to Him and confess our sins and ask for redemption.

As Christ said to the adulteress, "go, and sin no more." (John 8:11) When you go in prayer to the cross, confess your sins and ask forgiveness, you know your sins are forgiven. (I John 2:1-2) That does not mean you aren't a sinner. A sinner, by definition, is one who has sinned. The name sticks, but now you are recovering from your sinful life.

Let's consider the alcoholic. For any treatment to be effective, the person must first admit s/he is an alcoholic. Then, the alcoholic can follow the path to recovery through Alcoholics Anonymous (AA) or another treatment program. The person will still admit to you that s/he is an alcoholic, but now s/he uses the term "recovering alcoholic."

Those of us who have sought redemption and have been forgiven are still sinners, but now we are "recovering sinners." Unless we change our life patterns, we recognize we can slip easily into the sinful temptations. A recovering sinners' path to recovery may include prayer, regular attendance and meaningful participation in one's church, meet regularly with others struggling with sinful addictions, and seek the company of supportive associates in work and social life, to name a few.

Like the alcoholic, we must have a sincere desire, even commitment, to change our behavior to lead a Christ-like life.

With God's help, knowledge of right and wrong can be indelibly etched on our conscience, a small voice that speaks to us when we consider sinful actions or pursue impure thoughts.

Am I wrong to say we have all sinned? I don't think so! We can all be recovering sinners. We want to lead sinless lives, and do you know what happens? The more we try(do), the more successful we become. Just believe in Christ and go to Him for forgiveness.

Aim to make your path to forgiveness at the foot of the Cross less traveled, overgrown with vegetation due to lack of use.

> *He is able to save those who come to God through him because he is at the right hand of God and is always interceding for us.*
>
> *—Hebrews 7:25 NIV*

I was going to waste, but Jesus recycled me!

Day 17:

Negotiations

"All right," David replied, "but I will not negotiate with you unless you bring back my wife Michal, Saul's daughter, when you come." II Samuel 3:13

One of the experiences I enjoy most when on a cruise ship is shopping ashore. I like bargain hunting but try to limit myself to items I need, not just because it is a low price. Seaport vendors want to sell at a profit, that's why they are in business. They usually start with an inflated price because they know that a vast majority of buyers are accustomed to paying the marked price or asking price. The buyers from the States are not used to negotiating a price, occasionally to the point of being afraid they will insult the seller if they suggest a lower price.

As a buyer, I am willing to pay a fair price for an item that I want, but I dislike, even hate the seller trying to rip me off. Unfortunately, for bargain seekers, many cruise ship port merchants have agreed to maintain set prices and not negotiate. I have found no advantage in shopping around for bargains in those situations.

I relish the times when, like at a flea market, the price you pay is what you negotiate with the seller. When you are a captive of set market prices that are generally quite inflated, you pay more than what it's worth back home.

Negotiations are sort of like a game. The seller offers to sell at a specific price. The buyer responds with his counteroffer, and the seller may return with a reduced price, probably with complaints the buyer is trying to take advantage of him. In return, the buyer points out all the defects in the item that make it worth no more than his next offer.

The ball, so to speak, goes back and forth until the game ends; the deal is done, or the buyer or seller walks away. As the famous Kenny Rodgers song goes,

> "You got to know when to hold 'em,
> Know when to fold 'em,
> Know when to walk away,
> And know when to run."

The bible says, in Proverbs 20:14:

> *The buyer haggles over the price, saying,*
> *"It's worthless," then brags about getting*
> *a bargain!*

Personal and business relationships are like negotiations too. Have you ever been told to do something wrong, and you refused? Have you ever thought of negotiating a situation to make it half wrong? Is it a part of your moral structure to choose to do the right thing all the time? Or do you try to negotiate the right thing to make it almost right? Don't go there! It is time to walk away.

> *A wise person chooses the right road; a*
> *fool takes the wrong one.*
> —*Ecclesiastes 10:2*

It is hard to choose to do the right thing all the time, despite the temptations to do otherwise. That's a sign of integrity.

How is your integrity?

Let Christ guide your footsteps.

Day 18:

Listen for God

My child, pay attention to what I say.
Listen carefully to my words.
—Proverbs 4:20

I happen to believe that God talks to me. I think God talks to you too. **Bah! Humbug!** you say. How can that be? I believe that God is omnipotent and that by His very nature, He is omnipresent. That means that God is available, listening, and aware, everywhere at any time to anyone. It also means that we can communicate with God through various forms of prayer.

However, communication doesn't only mean sending messages; it means receiving them as well. It is a two-way process. God wants to hear from us, and for us to hear from Him.

Have you tapped into, or tuned into God yet? If you have severe doubts about this, I am not surprised. But, believe it or not, it happens all the time. Quite often, unfortunately, our communication antenna is not picking up God's frequency,

57

God could be speaking to you all the time; you just may not realize it.

Can you recall an instance in the last few days when the answer to a problem you had been struggling with suddenly became obvious? Did a possible course of action also become evident? That thought **out of the blue** (or sent from heaven) could have been God sending you a message.

Suppose you have a decision to make that can have troubling implications for you and your family. **When, all of a sudden, a solution to a vexing problem reveals itself, isn't God talking to you?**

> *For he is our God. We are the people he watches over, the flock under his care. If only you would listen to his voice today!*
> *—Psalm 95:7*

Some time ago, I enjoyed singing in the church choir. One evening, at choir practice, in the middle of one of a song, I received an inspiration that was the answer to a problem I was facing at that time. After this happened to me numerous times, I started taking a small pad and pen to choir practice so I wouldn't miss any part of God's messages.

Besides choir practice, there were other occasions like jogging when I felt God's inspirations. In all honesty, I must say that I hated to jog. I jogged because it was good for me, just like eating and sleeping. I jogged in the morning because I didn't want to go through my day knowing I would have to jog when I got home after work. Some people love it. That's fine for them. I hope they live to be 100.

But I digress. Often during my jog, I would get flashes of inspiration. Problems that were dogging me lessened as ways to resolve them came to mind. Yes, I believe God was talking to me.

No doubt, your experiences will differ from mine. You might get messages while you are cooking, mowing the grass, enjoying TV, driving in traffic, doing laps in the pool, *and at other times when you least expect them.*

Of course, don't confuse your hunches as God's messages when tempted to bet on RED, or ODD at the roulette table, or you feel a strong urge to fill an inside straight in a poker game. God doesn't play games, and **He isn't your gambling buddy!**

God speaks to us through a receptive heart. If you have hardened your heart as Pharaoh did, (But Pharaoh's heart was hard, and he would not listen, Exodus 8:19), then you won't recognize God's efforts to reach you.

Soften your heart and join countless others who benefit from a close relationship with God.

With all this in mind, can you recall times when you also received a divine inspiration?

The meek shoosh God, the wise heed Him.

Day 19:

Maria

My child, pay attention to what I say.
Listen carefully to my words.

—Proverbs 4:20

Some of the most important lessons I have learned in my life occurred when I was a member of a Vacation Bible School (VBS) team in Romania. The team leader, Stan, **who** interviewed me for the team, **said he** was looking for qualities like those found in Galatians 5:22-23, the **fruit of the spirit.** They are love, joy, peace, forbearance, kindness, goodness, faithfulness, gentleness, and self-control. And, of course, faith in Christ.

There was one quality he seemed to dwell on, and that was love. I asked him about that. He answered that when he was an elementary school principal, he would meet with the teachers at the end of each school year to assign students to the class for the following year. He said he tried to place children in a  class environment where they would have the most chance for both learning and behavior success. Whenever he would get to a "problem child" to be assigned to grade four, one teacher always said," I'll take him" (or her).

Stan told me that later, he quietly asked that teacher how she could take all those problematic students but never seemed to have the problems the other teachers had. The answer astounded him, but it was so obvious. She said,

"I just love 'em to death."

> *If I had the gift of prophecy, and if I*
> *understood all of God's secret plans and*
> *possessed all knowledge, and if I had such*
> *faith that I could move mountains, but*
> *didn't love others, I would be nothing.*
> —*I Corinthians 13:2*

I confessed that I'd feel like such a hypocrite. I am a sinner. How can I look a child in the eye and tell him how to live his life. Mine is a mess.

With a laugh, Stan explained,

"You may feel that's the case, but remember we are all a work in progress. None of us is free from sin. But we strive to avoid the sinful ways and exhibit the very qualities we want to impart to the children. Sincerity is the key here. Children spot a phony very quickly, but if you are sincere, you can be a real role model for the children at VBS."

Next, I asked Stan,

"How can I help when I don't know the language?" He told me it was not as big a problem as you might think. VBS isn't working with rocket science. Stan gave me this example. "One year, I was a helper in the Crafts section of VBS. Most children can mimic actions, instructions to do simple projects. Off to the side, I noticed a young gypsy girl, about 12 who was doing nothing. She was just looking around like she was lost. Naturally, I went to her, and through motions with my hands, and hers, she let me know she was stuck on the first step. The first step was to write her name on her project. She could not write her name. She said, "Maria."

I wrote "MARIA" on her project for her and gave her a little hug. She gave me a big smile that would melt a glacier. I could tell from the comments and giggles around the table, that Maria was frequently teased and rejected by her peers. Maria and I bonded at that point. It was moments like that that kept me wanting to return again and again, helping other Marias."

That's why he was a team leader.

It must have seemed to Stan that I was trying to avoid participating when I admitted I didn't know the Bible too well. I can't teach it.

"All I can say about that," answered Stan," is to make it a daily practice to spend some time with your Bible and make it (Jesus) your friend."

I am sure Stan had heard all these hesitations from applicants before, but he had good responses for them. During and after the VBS, I learned many useful lessons about myself.

Have you had unique experiences in your life? What did you learn from them? Did some of those experiences make you change some aspect of your life?

The bottom line to life, through the good experiences and the bad, is to keep your focus on God. You will be a better person for it.

> For I can do everything through Christ,
> who gives me strength.
> —Philippians 4:13

If God brings you to it, He will bring you through it.

Day 20:

Log on to God

Most hotels nowadays have at least one, and sometimes two or three computers set aside in the lobby or a designated room so guests can keep up with their world. A placard near the computer shows instructions and suggestions for use. For example:

This is terminal: HOTEL 1

The user name is: HOTEL 1

There is no password, just press Enter.

WARNING: These computers are monitored.

I have seen this kind of sign many times and often wondered if God had a computer; If so, how would His sign read?

To Log on to God:

This is terminal: HEAVEN 1

The user name is: PRAYER

There is no password, just begin.

WARNING: God is always listening. He is continually monitoring your thoughts, interests, plans, desires, needs, fears, anxieties. He is watching you all the time.

> *Nevertheless, listen to my prayer and my plea, O LORD my God. Hear the cry and the prayer that your servant is making to you.*
> *—2 Chronicles 6:19 NLT*

I got carried away with my fantasy and composed a list of things to keep in mind when communicating with God.

1. Know that God is listening. Don't insult his graciousness by shining him on. God understands:
    * Sincerity
    * Honesty
    * Expectations
    * Consistency
    * Devotion
    * Steadfast belief

2. Be careful what you pray for; you may not like God's answer. God answers when the time is right (His time).

3. Are your prayer unselfish ones, prayers for the benefit of others.

4. Prayers for yourself need to be selfless, not for power and riches, but self-fulfillment and physical and emotional well-being.

5. You can pray anytime, but make it part of your daily life, not just for special needs or occasions.

I'm not suggesting how you should pray; Jesus gave us a perfect example of that. I'm not suggesting what you should pray for. I am suggesting you make prayer a regular part of your life and life routine. It helps to keep your focus on Jesus, to use His words and actions as a guide on your path to being better persons.

While you are thinking about prayer, I challenge you to close your eyes and say a prayer keeping these suggestions in mind.

Praying can become a habit, a good habit. If praying isn't already, why not make praying a regular part of your life!

You faithfully answer our prayers with awesome deeds, O God our savior. You are the hope of everyone on earth, even those who sail on distant seas.

—Psalm 65:5 NLT

Get online with God. Download your worries.

Day 21:

In A Groove

Why do you do things the way you do them? Perhaps you had a grandmother like Gramma Bess. She was a good cook. She got squeals of delight when she made chocolate bread pudding with vanilla hard sauce or sweet potatoes with marshmallows. Gramma Bess made those culinary delights frequently because she got a favorable response from the eater.

That's why we do things the way we do them; because we are pleased with the results, others are pleased, and we are encouraged to continue doing things that way. Teachers try to instill that idea in the moral fabric of their students' minds.

Doing something a certain way all the time is okay, as is a habit of regular time with God through prayer, Bible reading, and other God-centered activities.

Individuals don't like to change their lifestyle. Yet sometimes change is forced upon them. They have no choice.

Recently everyone had to make do with the **"shelter in place"** or **lockdown** protocols put in place by the government. With certain exceptions, everyone had to stay in their home. That meant many changes in the way of life, worship, recreation, eating, and the use of leisure time; there was plenty of that.

It was a tragic situation for all. You may have been directly affected and knew the anguish of having to adapt to your new groove of life. Schools, factories, all kinds of stores, small and large, had to rethink their business model to survive economically.

During the COVID-19 Crisis, out of necessity, many new ways of doing things were attempted. People devised different ways to solve their problems. Interestingly, people found creative and innovative ways to meet their needs. Ask students about the innovations that took place because schools closed, and they had to learn in new and different ways. Teachers had to devise ways of teaching to keep the students interested and motivated.

Perhaps the COVID-19 Crisis was God's way of helping us get out of our rut, of getting us to take new approaches to problems, to start doing things a new and different way.

The physical church became a computer church with a software program called "Zoom."[1] We worshipped together but from home. David Irvine, Minister of Music, St Andrew Presbyterian Church, Sonoma in 2014, expressed it so well in verse three of his song, "The Church Has Left the Building."

> The church has left the building,
> Out of our walls we spring,
> We put our faith to action,
> Lord, let Your work be done,
> We are not proud,
> our heads are bowed,
> And sing of love out loud,
> The church has left the building,
> Good news to all we bring.

The setting in which we worship had to change, the

ways we communicate with each other had to change, but one thing that didn't change is our relationship with God! God still listens to our prayers. God still wants our love and adoration. God still looks to us to obey His commandments.

It is reassuring to know that God is with us, to guide us and nurture our well-being, our love for one another. People began caring more for the welfare of other people, calling them by phone or text to ensure they were safe and healthy.

Do you step up out of your rut to help someone in need by being there in text, word, or physical presence?

> *Then I heard the Lord asking, "Whom should I send as a messenger to this people? Who will go for us?" I said, "Here I am. Send me."*
>
> *—Isaiah 6:8*

Draw near to God, He will draw near to you.

Day 22:

The Beard

I have a white beard on my chin. I try to keep it trimmed to come to a point like a goatee, but I'm not always successful doing that. A beard is part of my persona, a part of a costume that, taken altogether, defines me. I think that my beard makes me look professorial, cultured, educated even inspiring like the old dons of Oxford and Cambridge strutting about in their caps and gowns.

Oxford Dons

Having a beard does have certain advantages. In a group where few other people have a beard, it makes me unique. Now, I don't need to be unique, but there are advantages to being unique. There are also disadvantages to being a little different.

The benefits are that people remember what I do. They remember my name. It's easy because I stand out in their mind as the old guy with the goatee.

Also, for the same reasons, it is a disadvantage because every little thing, every mistake I make, they know the guy with the weird beard. I'm not confused with other people. I'm like Charlie Chaplin (pictured to the left) with his unique mustache, cane, and waddle walk, President Franklin Delano Roosevelt with his long cigarette holder, or President Trump with his red tie.

Think about the little things that aren't so obvious? What things identify you as unique in some way? Do you have a manner of speech like a New England, Southern, or Texas accent? What about the things that can make you stand out, like your hairstyle, the type of clothing you wear, or the style of shoes like Wellington Boots. Maybe you have other traits that can identify you as only you.

Famous picture of President Franklin Denano Roosevelt smoking a cigarette in his famous cigarette holder. It is interesting that in recent years, our media has purged most of these pictures, due to our modern society's disdain for the use of tobacco products.

You can also be distinctive by the way you think, express yourself, and consistency in your choices, actions, and behaviors. When a person varies from their norm, people say," He/she's not him/herself today" Variations from the usual you are readily apparent.

Yes, it hard to do the wrong thing and not be noticed. People notice others who do the right thing too. My friend, Charles, always brings his Bible to church. It is a well-worn, obviously much used Bible. I never see him open it in church, but he has it anyway. I guess going to church with his Bible is a long time habit. I could spot him a mile away because of that trait.

> *Thank you for making me so wonderfully complex! Your workmanship is marvelous—how well I know it.*
> *—Psalm 139:14*

What are the various aspects of your life that let others know you walk with Christ? Are you identified as a person that loves Christ? Are you recognized as one who is seeking or has found the Lord? Do you strive to keep your life beyond reproach?

More of Jesus; less of me.

Day 23:

No Obligation

As I finished my morning Bible reading, I took what I thought was a piece of scrap paper and placed it in my Bible so I would know where to start reading the next day. Just as I closed the Bible, my eye caught a prominent phrase that grabbed my attention. I removed it and placed the Bible face down on the table to keep my place.

I focused my attention on the words **free gift**. Then I recalled the occasion when I got the piece of paper, the handout. At the time, I was a tourist visiting San Francisco. Walking around a Pier 39, a place best described as a tourist magnet, I was continually handed flyers touting a restaurant, store, or some **don't-miss-this** location.

discard later. All the flyers seemed to have essentially the same message. They offered some or all of the following benefits for visiting a particular location or business:

- FREE GIFT (always in large letters)
- Exceptional quality
- Outstanding value
- Special discounts
- Super low prices
- Worldwide service
- International reputation
- Locally operated

The free gift, I suspected, was something unique but of minimal value, **the hook** to reel me into the business from the crowded pedestrian sidewalk.

I chuckled to myself as I picked up the Bible and marked my place with the ad. I had just finished reading Luke 4:31 (NIV):

> *Then Jesus went to Capernaum, a town in Galilee, and taught there in the synagogue every Sabbath day.*

Again, I chuckled to myself.

I could picture the disciples standing around outside the synagogue, handing out single sheet ads encouraging people passing by to stop and listen to Jesus. Why? Look at these benefits:

- Jesus has a quality message.
- His words have infinite value.
- No surcharge, no minimum.
- He is the son of the one true God.
- His message is available worldwide.

+ He has been preaching everywhere.

+ He can perform miracles.

+ He has a rapidly expanding reputation

+ The message is free, no-obligation.

I laughed out loud as I visualized Jesus's disciples wandering through the countryside, passing out invitation messages to come and hear Jesus.

> One day as Jesus was preaching on the shore
> of the Sea of Galilee, great crowds pressed in
> on him to listen to the word of God.
> —Luke 5:1

Of course, all this is absurd, a product of my overactive, and occasionally mischievous imagination.

Then I thought, what would a promotional flyer say about me?

Ouch! That was a very sobering thought. True, I had been trying to walk with Christ, but my pace was slow, and I was falling behind. My efforts to talk about Christ were confused and frequently bordered on nonsense. Still, I was in the game. I want to do as much as I can to win men/women and children's souls for Christ. I pray my flyer will include:

+ He gives his all for Christ.

+ He does his best; Christ expects nothing less.

+ He embodies the fruit of the Spirit (love, joy, peace, forbearance, kindness, goodness, faithfulness) Galatians 5:22-23

+ He is like an olive tree flourishing in the house of God, trusting in God's unfailing love forever and ever. Psalm 52:8 (paraphrased)

What would you like your flyer to include?

_____

_____

_____

_____

_____

_____

_____

_____

_____

_____

Day 24:

The Big Idea

So, where did it all start? Who started this crazy idea? Can you imagine a church service where some members of the congregation and perhaps others, can join the worship service from home?

The pastor argued that the church needed a way to involve:

- the sick and infirm

- the homebound

- the elderly who can't drive to church.

- those who are intimidated by the church building itself, much less going inside.

- those who are concerned by their appearance, their dress, their speech, their language, or their color?

Individuals supporting the idea *could* see the need to make the word of God available to all the people despite physical circumstances or other limitations to the contrary. Also, they recognized the need  for everyone, believers, and non-believers to experience the word of God, the love of Jesus Christ.

Those opposing the idea expressed that it is not the way we do it. Church is in our glorious edifice, not a living room. We've always done it that way.

No need to change. So, it won't change until some irresistible force arises.

How can the "Church God" become a "Home God" too? Not just hearing a program on the radio or viewing an evangelist on the television, but worshipping using our computers as a location instead of a physical church building. How can the atmosphere of adoration and reverence to God that we feel in the physical church transfer to our living rooms at home?

The idea simmered until a method surfaced that would involve those at home as well as the worship leaders. Each would be able to see and interact with each other. All could feel involved.

> *Jesus looked at them intently and said,*
> *"Humanly speaking, it is impossible. But*
> *with God, everything is possible."*
> *—Matthew 19:26*

Then, someone recommended Zoom.

The pastor recognized the need and the possibilities of Zoom, but he hesitated because:

- Many are afraid to speak out and support the idea.
- People won't step forward and offer to help.
- They won't get off their duff and learn to use the app.
- They don't believe having an at-home church service is worth fighting the waves of opposition.

Despite his concerns, the pastor encouraged the church leaders to step forward using the story of Rev. Frank Norris, the pastor of First Baptist Church in Fort Worth, Texas for over forty years. Pastor Norris did not need to experience a COVID-19 epidemic to see the possibilities of radio in 1920.[1]

---

[1] Though he and his church did experience the Spanish Flu epidemic that struck the United States in 1919-1921. It is unknown as to whether the effects of that flu epidemic was a consideration in their decision to use radio.

(before many people even owned or could afford radios) Radio allowed people to go to church, even when they stayed at home. His church bought a small transmitter and started broadcasting his sermons to the Dallas-Fort Worth area on a daily basis, effectively allowing people to experience church at home.

The church's radio program was so succcessful that even members of the Roman Catholic faith, who were forbidden, at the time, to listen to Protestant ministers, turned on their radios and started listening. If the priest happened to call, it was a small matter to simply shut off the radio. Of course, if the priest's visit was a short one, the people might not appreciate missing half of Rev. Norris' message waiting for the vaccuum tubes in the radio to warm up.

Using the example of Rev. Norris and other ministries, the spirit of the Lord started to move the congregation; maybe hostile at first, then reluctantly, then accepting and finally embracing the concept enthusiastically. They began to see the possibilities for their church using Zoom in 2020.[2]

Eventually, the body of the church relished what it saw happening to those who must, or chose, to stay homebound.

- They learned the Lord still loves them.
- They learn what it is like to show concern for others and to share the love of Jesus Christ through others.
- They realized it is not the location, the mind, or the body but the heart of the people that brings the

[2] Please refer to my other footnote about Zoom on page xx and how it could work for your church.

body and minds of believers together as a church, wherever they are.

> *But ye shall receive power, after that the*
> *Holy Ghost has come upon you: and ye shall*
> *be witnesses unto me both in Jerusalem, and*
> *in all Judaea, and in Samaria, **and unto***
> ***the uttermost part of the earth.***
> —*Acts 1:8 NLT*

Yes, even at home, or on vacation. Now the fellowship of God can be with you, always, even to the ends of the earth.

A rose in a locked garden still has a delightful aroma.

Day 25:

Check Your Caller ID

Telephone answering machines are a wonderful invention. So is "Caller ID." That is caller identification, so you can see who is calling you. Then you have to decide whether to answer the call or not.

If the caller is someone you know and enjoy conversing with, then you answer. If it a family member, the chances are high that you will lift the receiver and give a warm greeting. Ok, maybe not for Aunt Mabel, who is always complaining about something and wants to bend your ear for sympathy and maybe your support.

Suppose the phone screen says," Unknown Caller." Chances are you will refuse to answer that call. It is likely a robot call or one made by a telemarketer for a business, a political organization, or a fundraiser for organizations like The Sacred Order of Heavenly Frogs. My policy is  never to respond to appeals for money over the phone. The causes may sound good, but there are a lot of scams out there too, so I prefer to be on the safe side.

You probably get calls like that too.

My phone number is on the **do not call list**, so I remind the caller of that fact. The caller blatantly tells me that their organization is "exempt," and my threats of reporting the caller to the Federal Communication Commission (FCC) will fall on deaf ears. Occasionally I errantly answer the phone before I check the caller ID screen, and when I find out I don't want to talk to the caller, I just hang up.

A big give away is the question, "Is this (your first name)?" You see, they are trying to establish familiarity. One friend of mind responds with: "Sorry, he's on the roof trying to overcome his fear of heights." That usually ends the conversation.

Another friend of mine never answers his phone right away. He has recorded a message,

"Sorry to miss your call, but my wife and I are busy expressing our true love for each other. Leave your number and the purpose of your call. I'll get back to you as soon as I can. (short pause) It might be a while."

Suppose one day your phone rings, and you check the ID. It is a call from God. If it is actually from God, you can't run and hide. God is everywhere. So, you answer the phone.

What do you say?

"Hello, God..."

Sounds too familiar... You consider,

"Hello Father..."

But that sounds too catholic. How about,

"This is Frank speaking. How can I help you, God?"

No. That's too formal and business-like. In desperation, you blurt out,

"Hello, this is Frank. I know I have sinned and I'm really sorry. I promise I won't do it again. Please forgive me."

Perhaps He is calling about the lustful thoughts I had yesterday.

"I know I need to struggle against such thoughts," I admitted.

"I beg your forgiveness. Dear God, I confess I spoke ill of my neighbor, but I repent and ask you to forgive me."

Then you get the reason God's reaching out to you.

"Hello, Frank. I was just checking on you. I haven't heard from you for quite a while. I miss our regular conversations. Perhaps they will help you with those moral and behavioral concerns you have. Please contact me as soon as you are ready."

Are you ready to talk to God today? What will you say? God is a loving, forgiving God. He means what he says, is trustworthy, everlasting, and keeps his word. He wants to be your constant and closest friend.

Maybe it is time for you to call God again. Make sure His Caller ID says **your name**, not **Unknown Caller**?

Feeling stressed?
Talk with God.
Get blessed!

Day 26:

Sayings, Quotes, and Proverbs

Proverbs are expressions that have a timeless, instructive, meaningful value. There are many synonyms for proverbs like axiom, saying, adage, saw, maxim, motto, aphorism, epigram, gnome, dictum, precept, slogan, truism, platitude, and cliché.

Many proverbs are just common sense; others *are* mundane, and a few are immoral. They can be read or said without regard to culture or nationality. Proverbs are not promises and are generally true, but not always.

Whenever I find myself down in the doldrums, I seek refuge and help from the Bible. Sometimes I go to the Book of James, other times to Psalms. One of my favorites and a favorite of many people is the Book of Proverbs. There I find thoughts that make me chuckle, inspire me, maybe make me feel sad; they tend to help my every mood.

The name closely associated with Proverbs is King Solomon. Biblical historians attribute 3,000 proverbs either collected or written by him. They became widespread over several centuries. Eventually, King Hezekiah made a sincere effort to gather the sayings that are in the Bible as the Book of Proverbs.

If Solomon were collecting proverbs today, some of his sayings might include:

A wise teacher heeds his own words.

A wise man wears his preventive mask; a fool displays his face with no concern for others.

Sheltering in place is like hibernation, but you gain weight.

A lazy man is as useful as a fork with no tongs.

It is better to enjoy solitude than live next to a 24-hour night club.

Staying too long in the sun is like drinking too much wine; both lead to a painful, restless night of regret.

Separation can be good for a lover's heart if the beats of affection are enduring.

New challenges foster new solutions.

Satisfaction with the present shows the lack of a plan for the future.

Fair Winds and following seas are like blessings from God.

Solomon inspired me to start collecting sayings that I felt were worth remembering. I decided to try writing some proverbs too.

This book contains part of them, but I also found some on Facebook as inspirational sayings. More sayings appear in the chapter at the end of this book.

I pray you will remember some of them and be inspired. May these quotes encourage you to learn something new and always push the boundaries.

> *Let those who are wise understand these things. Let those with discernment listen carefully. The paths of the LORD are true and right, And righteous people live by walking in them. But in those paths, sinners stumble and fall.*
>
> *—Hosea 14:9 (NLT)*

A word to the wise – should be heeded.

Day 27:

Take Off Your Mask

Remember costume parties? You know, a party where everyone dresses in clothes that resemble a well know fictional or real person. And of course, one must wear a mask.

Whatever the costume, part of the fun was trying to guess who it was. Because the height, weight, eye color, and hair color gave significant clues, some people were easy to identify. Other clues were the person's voice, the way they walked, the appearance of their hands, and the shape of their ear.

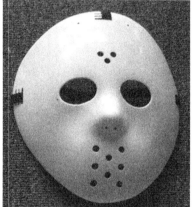

In other words, it is tough to hide who you are. Despite your costume, people will guess your name. Even a block away, you can tell who a person is by the way they walk, the hairstyle, or the type of clothing.

But I'm not referring to the physical you. Take away the physical attributes and costume, who are you? A social scientist might say people are known by:

+ What they do.
+ What they say,
+ What others do to or say about them.

None of these items mention **appearance**. They refer to character, honesty, and integrity. We can get character guidance from at least two sources in the Bible. The Apostle Paul gives guidance in the Fruit of the Spirit:

> *But the Holy Spirit produces this kind of fruit in our lives: love, joy, peace, patience, kindness, goodness, faithfulness, gentleness, and self-control. There is no law against these things!*
> —Galatians 5:22-23 NLT

The Apostle Peter says it another way;

> *In view of all this, make every effort to respond to God's promises. Supplement your faith with a generous provision of moral excellence, and moral excellence with knowledge, and knowledge with self-control, and self-control with patient endurance, and patient endurance with godliness, and godliness with brotherly affection, and brotherly affection with love for everyone.*
> —2 Peter 1:5-7 (NLT)

I'd wager you follow similar guidelines when you form opinions about pastors, politicians, and presidents or leaders of businesses, community organizations, and clubs, for example.

When you believe no one will see you, do you act differently? When you are the buffet table, do you dare to take an extra deviled egg? Or linger by the guacamole dip a little too long?

Do you act the same way to a salesperson as you do to the beggar holding a sign on the street corner? Do you react to people at work the same as you do at a neighborhood barbeque? Who is the real you? Is the real you the person you want you to be? That God wants you to be?

Today, now, **take your mask off.**

Are your traits of a Christian character consistent? Parents know that to discipline a child successfully, they must be consistent. Behaving consistently in all situations shows that a person is comfortable with himself. He doesn't have to pretend to be something he isn't. Some call it: **integrity**. Whatever you call it, how do you match up?

Are you the real you all the time? Do people respect you because they know who and what you are?

Do you behave towards others as you would toward God?

You can fool all the people some of the time, and you can fool some people all the time. But you can never fool God!

Day 28:

Victim or Victorious

For several years Tom, the Mission Pastor at a rural church near San Francisco, and six members of his congregation had joined people from a church In Los Angeles on a mission to conduct a Vacation Bible School (VBS) in Romania.

This year, to get ahead of the game, Tom had held a few meetings to prepare lesson plans, accumulate supplies, and learn some phrases in Romanian. Then he received a phone call from Paul, the chief mission leader in Los Angeles. That call hit Tom like a giant wave crashing him against a rocky shore. Paul said he had severe health problems and couldn't lead the team this year.

Panic time for Tom...

How can he inform his little contingent that, after all their planning and work, the mission is canceled? He felt helpless and miserable.

Depressed and discouraged, Tom called the team together and sadly explained that due to Paul's health, they would not be holding a VBS in Romania.

Instead of grumbling, the response was,

"Why? Isn't there a way we can do it with six people instead of 30? Suppose we... and ideas started to flow freely. Somehow this dedicated group was going to present a VBS in Romania! I firmly believe the Lord showed them the way.

Turn the situation into something good, maybe even better than you hoped for in the beginning.

Tom knew his team had a challenging task. They had never conducted the VBS with so few people before. So, what did they do? They changed the focus and role of the team.

Past teams had volunteers from the host church support them by translating and assisting with the Crafts, Recreation, Bible Study, and Praise Worship. This year the team would train the volunteers to take the lead roles. The team would give support. Everyone understood they were plowing new ground and were full of anticipation of what the new crop would yield.

Their efforts were so successful that they changed their whole mindset and mode of operation for future VBS programs.

> *The Lord Is Good, a strong refuge when*
> *trouble comes. He is close to those who*
> *trust in him.*
> *—Nahum 1:7 NLT*

Even when things go wrong, it doesn't have to feel like the end of the world. Never be too proud to admit that you've got a problem. Don't hesitate to call for ideas, assistance from your friends, and associates.

Above all, don't be like a 5-year-old child, who says, "Leave me alone. I can do it myself."

Let the Lord in and accept His help. He's just waiting for you to ask Him!

> *But blessed is the one who trusts in the*
> *Lord, whose confidence is in him. They*
> *will be like a tree planted by the water*
> *that sends out its roots by the stream. It*
> *has no fear when heat comes; its leaves are*
> *always green. It has no worries in a year of*
> *drought and never fails to bear fruit.*
> *—Jeremiah 17:7-8 NIV*

Life can be static...
Growth is optional...
Choose wisely!

Day 29:

Helping Others Helps Yourself

Recently I had a bad case of the BLAHS. I had faced one depressing thing after another. My outlook was pretty grim. For some unexplained reason, my thoughts shifted to a time years ago when I had similar feelings.

I was a midshipman stationed aboard the destroyer the USS *Johnston* (DD821), approaching the dock at the now infamous Guantanamo Navy Base, Cuba. An authoritative voice on the ship's loudspeaker asked for volunteers to load supplies. I

Author Photo of USS *Johnston*, June 5, 1955 at Newport, Virginia

thought, *After the work party finished loading, we'll get our liberty ahead of rest of the anxious crew.* So, I volunteered.

Cuba, in July, is hot, very hot... Loading supplies made it seem even hotter, and people seemed to work at a slower pace in the heat. By the time we got off loading duty, the rest of the ship's crew was long gone, disappeared over the sandy shore road to partake of the delights at the Navy Exchange (store).

I quickly changed into the liberty uniform and went topside and, as protocol required, asked permission to go ashore from the officer of the deck. My request to go ashore was granted, so I headed, all alone up a dusty dirt road.

Talk about the Blahs. I was all alone with no idea where anything was located or how I was going to get there except walk in the burning, dusty heat.

Resigned to my fate, and frankly feeling very sorry for myself, I slowly started down the road.

Parked off to the side of the road (I can still picture it so clearly) was a maroon Mercury

Author Photo

convertible. I had almost walked past it when I heard,

"Young man, can you help me?"

I turned around and saw the driver, a woman with a pleading expression on her face. I thought to myself, *another thing to prevent me from getting to the Exchange. Oh, well, it is probably so crowded by now, a few minutes won't make any difference.*

The lady explained that her nephew was aboard one of the three ships at the dock, but she didn't know which one. She was supposed to meet him. Would I please check and see if he is still aboard any of the ships.

I searched through all three ships but couldn't find her nephew. When I reported back to her, she decided the nephew must have gone to the Exchange. She invited me to ride with her to the Exchange to look for him. I began to enjoy myself, riding, not walking, the welcome cooling wind blowing through my buzz-cut hair. I felt like a king in his chariot.

We found her nephew. All was well. Other good things continued to happen, all because I had removed myself from my funk and got outside my miserable being to help someone.

I think of that occasion often. Whenever I feel the blahs coming on, I look for a way to do something for someone, to get outside my selfish self and do something for others. You know, it works. Maybe that is why I genuinely enjoy my work for the Lord.

All my time working with others is really outside myself, the THEM has replaced the ME, and I have much joy in the Lord.

Maybe you are at a time in your life when your life seems a perpetual blah. It happens to others more often than you think. I was fortunate. God gave me this lesson when I was a young man. And it has continued to help me all my life.

Don't wait for the blahs; help someone today! Anticipating doing good things for the Lord works too.

> For even the Son of Man did not come
> to be served, but to serve, and to give his
> life as a ransom for many."
> —Mark 10:45 NIV

Want JOY?
Give it to others
in abundance.
Make their day!

Reflections

Day 30:

Hey, God's Talking to You

You say,
"bake, take, lake, sake, make, fake, rake, wake, cake."
I say,
"Whaaat?"

I hear you talking, but I can't understand. Those words all sound the same to me. Call it:

- a hearing deficit,
- a hearing disorder,
- an auditory dysfunction,
- a sound wave impediment,
- a little deaf,
- whatever is the current term.

Simply put, I have a hard time discerning the consonant sounds for b, t, l, m, f, w, h, and c.

I have become adept at nodding appropriately, smiling, occasionally grunting to show I am listening, even though I do not understand what is said. In a normal conversation, when I don't understand a word, I try to get the context so I can figure out what was said. But by then, the talker is two verbal paragraphs ahead, and that means I am totally lost.

Over time, I have come to realize that much of what I try to hear is meaningless small talk. It makes no difference whether I understand or not. I have become skilled at saying innocuous terms like,

"really, you don't say,"

or *smile and laugh* to give the impression I am mentally engaged. I feel like a young man on a deadbeat date attempting to be polite.

I try to avoid such situations.

However, a big problem remains. I cannot always understand my wife.

Some people would look at that as a blessing, but when my wife says something, it is usually something that requires my attention.

I acquired a small microphone my wife can clip to her blouse. It transmits her voice to my hearing aids. Now when she even whispers, fusses at the dishwasher, dryer, or another source of frustration, I hear her loud and clear.

But I don't need the latest technical device to hear God. I believe what God says is important. I want to hear and understand God. My problem is that I am not always on God's frequency. Thinking in retrospect, I can recall times when I think God was trying to get through to me, but I just wasn't listening. Even worse, I was either ignoring his messages, or too involved with myself to pay attention to His message.

He often gives guidance:

+ about things to do or not to do.
+ about things to say or not say.
+ about words to use or not use.
+ whether to write or not write.
+ whether to act or not to act.

Maybe you can recall times when, for example, you have felt God nudging you to tear up an angry letter or delete an email you wrote in haste.

Yes, God is always with us, trying to help us to make wise decisions. The closer we are to God, the more we decide to do things God's way rather than our way. Be alert for His messages. He may be softly whispering to you now!

Tune your ears to wisdom, and concentrate on understanding.
—Proverbs 2:2 NLT

Many people only pray to <u>ask for things</u>. Get His attention with <u>praise</u> and <u>thanks</u> as well.

Day 31:

They Shall Know You by Your Zeal

Recently, I received an email from a friend who sends me military associated tidbits that he feels might interest me. This tidbit was the obituary of a veteran citing actions he took during World War II to save lives and win the war.

On May 23, 1944, near Cerano, Italy, Van T. Barfoot set out alone to flank German machine gun positions from which gunfire was raining down on his fellow soldiers. His advance took him through a minefield. Having survived that, he proceeded to single-handedly take out three enemy machine gun positions and return with 17 prisoners of war. As if that weren't enough for a day's work, he later took on and destroyed three German tanks sent to retake the machine gun positions.

T/Sgt. Van T. Barfoot

This 21-year-old warrior was later awarded the Congressional Medal of Honor for his significant and brave valor during World War II. He was then promoted Second Lieutenant and continued fight in the War.

He went on to serve his country in Korea and Vietnam. Eventually, Colonel Barfoot retired to a home in a community that was governed by the Homeowners Association (HOA) rules and restrictions.

Col. Barfoot knew the HOA rules, so he applied for a permit to raise a 21-foot flagpole in his front yard so he could fly the flag for which he proudly fought. He was turned down but put up the flagpole anyway. The Homeowners' Association (HOA) threatened him with court action. This patriotic, decorated veteran stood fast.

This story received national TV and press coverage. Eventually, the HOA relented allowed the pole to stand so Old Glory can fly gracefully in the wind over his home

So, what is the significance of this story? Why include it here? I was impressed by not only the bravery of this man but his fervent zeal for his country. In the war, his life was on the line. At home, he risked being ostracized by his friends and neighbors and shunned by the community. Yet he stood firm.

Just imagine a world where all Christians had the zeal for the Lord that Colonel Barfoot had for his country. This verse from Romans 12:11 comes to mind:

> *Never be lacking in zeal, but keep your*
> *spiritual fervor, serving the Lord.*

We don't face the decision that the Christian Romans did when they refused to pay tribute to one of the Cesears who decided he was a god. They knew that their choice would result in a martyr's death.

I'm not asking you to die, but do you readily identify as a Christian. Do you, sometimes alone, speak out for Christian causes, for what is right, for what would glorify Christ? Or do you try to remain anonymous and fade into the masses who hesitate or fear to express their feelings?

Life gives us those challenges every day. Are you up to the challenge? Do you have the Christian zeal?

Don't let fear and insecurity silence your obligation to speak out and be heard.

Day 32:

They Will Know Your LOVE

Last week, I attended a memorial service for a dear friend. When I was a young man, such services were called "funerals." I guess that term seemed too deathly, so now it is termed a "memorial service" or sometimes a "celebration of life." For what is usually a sad occasion, I like the latter use better.

The pastor conducting the service asked the congregation of mourners to call out one or two words that describe the departed. There were many attributes called out in response, over twenty, including thoughtful, forgiving, loving, resourceful, hard worker, a leader, compassionate, and the like.

Yes, I called out a response too, and thought when my time comes, what will people speak out about me? How will I be remembered? What will be my legacy?

We don't have to die to be remembered. We are remembered in many and varied ways all the time. Think of the roles we play in our family, neighborhood, church, business and social organizations, workplace, friendships, and acquaintances. We are remembered by what we do and say in relating to others and life situations all the time.

The Bible has several places where it says we will be remembered. We will be remembered by our actions, by our joy, by our compassion, by our faith, and above all, by our love.

In English, love is expressed in one word, in Greek by at least four words because there can be different kinds of love. Specifically: *Agape* – love; *Eros* – passionate love; **Phila** – brotherly love; and *Xenia* – charitable, giving love. I like

Apostle Paul's definition from 1 Corinthians 13:

> *Love is patient; love is kind. It does not envy; it does not boast; it is not proud. It does not dishonor others; it is not self-seeking; it is not easily angered; it keeps no record of wrongs. Love does not delight in evil but rejoices with the truth. It always protects, always trusts, always hopes, always perseveres.*

Love is mentioned 686 times in the NIV Bible (Bible Gateway). I think God considers love a fundamental, necessary part of life.

Paul's emphasizes the importance of love in 1 Corinthians 13,

> *If I speak in the tongues of men or of angels, but do not have love, I am only a resounding gong or a clanging cymbal. If I have the gift of prophecy and can fathom all mysteries and all knowledge, and if I have a faith that can move mountains, but do not have love, I am nothing. If I give all I possess to the poor and give over my body to hardship that I may boast, but do not have love, I gain nothing.*

LOVE. That's what life boils down to, isn't it; our Love of the Lord and the Love of others.

> *Love the LORD your God with all your heart and with all your soul and with all your strength.*
> —*Deuteronomy 6:5*

I pray we are remembered, as the famous Christian song says,

> We are one in the Spirit,
> we are one in the Lord
> We are one in the Spirit,
> we are one in the Lord
> And we pray that our unity
> will one day be restored
> And they'll know we are Christians
> by our love, by our love
> **Yeah they'll know we are Christians
> by our love.**[1]

Love is acceptably expressed in many ways; by body language, a hug, a touch, by speaking in a loving tone and in speaking and writing using loving words and phrases that send the message that you genuinely care and love the person or group. The list of ways to express love is endless.

True love is expressed best in many ways and repeatedly! A child, spouse, family member, or anyone will never tire of knowing you love them!

So now the challenge... Can you do better in maintaining your loving relationships?

The more love we give, the more love we get in return.

Want more love?
Love more!

Day 33:

Cat in the Tree

I grew up in a neighborhood with a lot of trees and a lot of cats. That meant a cat frequently got stuck in a tree. When a cat gets stuck in a tree, they let you know about it. The usual meek meow suddenly becomes like a voracious roar that attracts a crowd of children, and some adults. They gather around and try to coax the cat out of the tree, but with no success.

Sooner or later, someone will call the fire department. A fire engine will arrive, and a fireman will climb the ever-present ladder and rescue the cat.

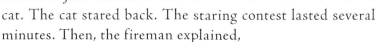

One day, when the firetruck arrived, the fireman got out and stood under the tree. He just stared at the cat. The cat stared back. The staring contest lasted several minutes. Then, the fireman explained,

"Now the cat knows that I know s/he is in the tree. What that cat is going to find out is that I am NOT going to do anything about it."

He then told everyone they needed to leave the cat and to go home, and he left. The cat, knowing it would get no more attention, found a way to get down by herself. It works. Have you ever seen a dead cat in a tree?

*I will lead the blind by ways they have
not known, along unfamiliar paths I will
guide them; I will turn the darkness into
light before them and make the rough
places smooth. These are the things I
will do; I will not forsake them.*
—Isaiah 42:16 NIV

Harry, my roommate in college, had deplorable study habits. At exam time, he would realize he had got himself into a mess (like the cat) and would stay up his tree cramming, complaining that he should have studied throughout the semester, and not waited until the end. Eventually, Harry owned up to his problem realizing that **only he could do something about it**. Understanding that most of the time, nobody is going to rescue you... it is up to you to solve your own problems. Overcoming problems is one way we learn about how to live life.

So, if you ever feel like the cat stuck in the tree, try these suggestions next time:

+ Don't panic, that makes your brain immobile and/or leads to quick hasty, not well-considered decisions.

+ Take a few moments to pray. This time with the Lord gives you time to gather your thoughts and approach your situation more at ease and objectively. You never know... He might suggest something you never thought of!

+ Consider your courses of action, jump down, climb down facing down, climb down facing up (backing down), look for another place or places to jump. In other words, see alternative solutions.

+ Consider the pros and cons of each course of action.

+ Try to erase the fear factor. Climbing down is much scarier than climbing up.

+ Choose the one that seems most likely to be successful. The important thing is to take action.

> **"Don't miss the joy of success because of the possibility of failure."**
>
> —*Warren Jaycox*

Sometimes, God will put a Goliath in your life so you can find the David within you.

Day 34:

The Great Commission

In this morning's paper, there was a quote, " If a man says he will do something, he will do it. No need to remind him every six months." Yeah, sure. Jesus knew human nature better than that. In the **Good News**, His message was important enough to be quoted, not only by Matthew but by Mark, Luke and John as well.

Jesus came and told his disciples, "I have been given all authority in heaven and on earth. Therefore, go and make disciples of all the nation, baptizing them in the name of the Father and the Son and the Holy Spirit. Teach these new disciples to obey all the commands I have given you. And be sure of this; I am with you always, even to the end of the age.

—Matthew 28:18-20

And then he told them, "Go into all the world and preach the Good News to everyone. Anyone who believes and is baptized will be saved. But anyone who refuses to believe will be condemned.
—Mark 16:15-16

It was also written that this message would be proclaimed in the authority of his name to all the nations.
—Luke 24:47

Again, he said, "Peace be with you. As the Father has sent me, so I am now sending you.
—John 20:21

Is Jesus trying to tell us something?

As I sat in my local church pew, I wondered how all that could pertain to me. That's for the missionaries to do. We write them letters of support and send financial assistance, but what more do they want.

Whoa! It isn't what THEY want; it is what God wants. So I began thinking, "What is God's plan for me? I felt good about my Christian life. After all:

- I tried to obey all his commandments. Some of them were pretty tough, but I did my best.
- I went to church every Sunday. (Well, almost every Sunday)
- I participated in the youth group and later the adult activities at the church.
- I gave an offering every Sunday, eventually managing to tithe.

- ✦ I said my prayers every night although usually some memorized rhyme as I learned as a child, but later tried to be more personal in my prayers.
- ✦ I was tolerant and respectful to all races, denominations, sexes male and female or whatever...

Sure, I did a commendable job of playing the Christian role. Then God challenged me to Get Out of the Pew and Start to Do!

Right there in front of me in the church bulletin, were places where God needed me. Volunteers were needed to help with Sunday School. Join the men's club, help organize a Vacation Bible School (VBS), or ask to be on the church leadership team. Do I need to sit and write those verses from Matthew, Mark, Luke, and John 100 times, so they will be emblazoned on my mind? Of course not! **God is showing me some ways to GO AND DO!**

What is God pointing you to be or do to serve Him?

Whatever you do, do everything for the glory of God.

I Corinthians 10:31

Day 35:

The Long Good-Bye

Yesterday, I went to see my wife. She is confined in a nearby but lovely residential care home. It is like a nursing home, but with fewer patients. When I pay my visits, I routinely read to her, show her family pictures, and pray with her... all with "pandemic restrictions."

We were outside enjoying the delightfully warm summer day. The flowers were full of scent and blooming, the trees in full leaf against the almost cloudless sky.

Nearby, not much over six feet away, was an elderly man and his wife, both adorned with the mandatory masks our state now requires all of us to wear, due to the COVID-19 pandemic. They were just sitting, looking at each other. He was talking softly, and I could detect he was weeping, most of the tears hidden behind his mask. The attendant explained to me that they have been married for 63 years. I sensed his yearning to hold her, to caress her, to kiss her, even only hold her hand. I detected her gaze wandering from time to time, but his eyes stayed on hers.

As I watched the hapless man attempted to communicate with his partner of over six decades, I felt, within my soul that there was, within his wife, a spark of understanding, that she sensed, deep inside of her that he still loved her, still cared for her and that he would be with her until they said their final good-byes.

I wondered, why are they being deprived of expressing the best medicine we have for people who are hurting or ill... that is Love... Fully-expressed with legal prohibitions. There must be some way that those who make the restrictive decisions can devise a way to allow the last days of that man and wife to be together if only to hold hands. There is a lot of love in just a touch.

Just before I left a few minutes later, the aged fellow got up, gave a departing wave, blew her a kiss, and then slowly walked, hunched over to his car. Not long after that, when I departed, he was still in his car, staring straight ahead, almost catatonic. He had a handkerchief in his hand. I'd bet he had been dreaming of the many happy long-gone days with his lovely wife. I got in my car and did the same.

I knew what he was feeling. I felt that way too. When his wife finally dies, she will be gone. But in the meantime, she is gone, yet is still here.

Not to get scientific or psychological... but what I was experiencing was love in action. To digress a moment, Dr. Abraham Maslow, an American psychologist, in his famous bestselling 1954 book, *Motivation and Personality*, defined five categories of basic human needs: Physiological, Safety, Love, Esteem, and Self-Actualization.

The first two involved the care and feeding, along with a safe environment. The residential care facility met them. The top two, Esteem and self-actualization, were beyond the understanding and comprehension of the patients with diminished mental capacity. That left Love. That's all the old man could offer his wife, but he could not fully express it.

They say it "takes one to know one." I can understand the emotional suffering of the thousands of people who must sit by and watch their loved ones drift away alone. Both the patient and the visitor are victims of a pandemic- caused loneliness.

I was fortunate enough to be with both my parents when they died. I could hold them and make sure they knew I loved them. I know of other cases where family members and friends would pray and sing favorite hymns as their loved one slowly passed away.

> *This is why I weep and my eyes*
> *overflow with tears. No one is near to*
> *comfort me, no one to restore my spirit.*
> —*Lamentations 1:16*

Someday, hopefully soon, it will be possible to screen all visitors to nursing home patients for possible infections like COVID-19 and get results within a few minutes. Imagine the joy of the visitors, amid the sadness, to be able to express, personally, their love, encouragement, and maybe hope for the patients. There will joy in the patients, too, being able to return the expressions of love being poured forth upon them.

> *Shout for joy, you heavens; rejoice, you*
> *earth; burst into song, you mountains!*
> *For the Lord comforts his people and will*
> *have compassion on his afflicted ones.*
> —*Isaiah 49:13*

Won't you join with the Lord and strive to ease the emotional pain of loneliness in others like that old couple? Why not take a moment to give some love and encouragement, make a phone call, write a letter, send a card or an email. Let them know they are not alone, that you care!

Life isn't about waiting for the storm to pass, it is about learning to dance in the rain.

Reflections

Day 36:

Memorable Collection

Through the 35 episodes in this book, there have been stories to make you think, to make you feel inspired, and to alert you to the role God can play in your life.

There is always more to say than space to say it, so this final chapter is a catch-all. Below are more proverbs, sayings, and quotes. As you come across quotes you wish to remember over the years, use the additional space to write them. Or you can copy them and stick them to a mirror, desk, or refrigerator. Share those that touch your heart on social media or frame them to hang on your wall.

- *It is what it is, expresses no hope for change.*
- *A cheerful person is like a beautiful everblooming rose.*
- *A man standing still may not be inert; he may be cautiously alert.*
- *It is better to follow instructions for your trip to survival than to be standing on the pier as the boat pulls away.*
- *As your image in the mirror can turn ugly, so can your garden without care get weeds.*
- *It is better to switch the TV off than to suffer incessant talking heads.*
- *The weak and foolish dislike, even hate, a successful man, but a strong leader will endure and excel.*
- *It is better to perceive than to observe. The godly man celebrates life; The sinner mopes in shame.*

- *It is better to fear God and celebrate in heaven than to flaunt God and wither in hell.*
- *God's laws direct our way to a good life; choosing a different path ends in a pit of despair.*
- *Proving the naysayers wrong is one of life's pleasures.*
- *Success comes from defeating your fear and insecurity.*
- *Fools see only storm clouds: Wise men see the beginning of rainbows.*
- *If it ain't broke, don't fix it.*
- *Better to carry an umbrella than to curse the rain.*
- *A good listener makes a smarter person*
- *The finger of success should point to others; the finger of failure should point to you.*
- *Fools say it can't be done; the wise say it hasn't been done yet.*
- *Fools are the ones things happen to; It's the wise who make things happen.*
- *A moving car is hard to stop; a stopped car is hard to move.*
- *When all else fails, read the instructions.*

Reflections

126

About the Author

Warren Jaycox was born in Baltimore, Maryland. He earned his B.A. from Rice University in 1954, his M.A. from California State University-Los Angeles in 1959, and his Ed.D. degree from the University of Southern California in 1967.

He served his country in the Marine Corps for thirty years, combined active and reserve duty. He retired as a Colonel in 1984.

Dr. Jaycox has served as president of local Optimist and Rotary clubs, served on local civic boards and commissions, and organized and operated several independent businesses.

During his vigorious life, he has held private pilot license.

He holds Life Elementary, Secondary, Administrative, and Pupil Personnel Credentials from the State of California, spending 18 wonderful years in the field of education. He started out teaching grades kindergarten through junior college. Later on, he served in administrative roles as an elementary principal and school superintendent.

In Romania, he organized the volunteers in Codlea as Vacation Bible School (VBS) Disciples. He and his team from Sonoma trained them to organize and conduct a VBS themselves. Since then, the VBS Disciples have accepted their great commission by starting VBS programs in other churches in their area of Romania.

Based on his work with VBS and service to bring others to the love of Christ, The Christian National Church ordained him in 2016. The same year, he established Disciples for Christ, a mission church to support VBS activities overseas.

In his spare time, he enjoys reading, playing Bridge, solving Sudoku puzzles, and finding out why something doesn't work, work as well as it should, or can work better. He and his wife of 63 years have three adult children, five adult grandchildren, and one great-grandchild. He now resides in Sonoma, California.

Thank You Note!

Thank you for reading my book!

If this book helped you in one way or another,
I would love to know more!

So, please, leave your feedback in a review on Amazon
and don't hesitate to contact me via e-mail at:
warren.jaycox@whitecottagepublishing.com

Thank you! Be Blessed!

Printed in Great Britain
by Amazon

26633989R00079